Poems and Recitations

Best Wishes

The bells are ringing.
They seem to say,
"Best wishes to all
This Christmas Day!

—*Robert Colbert*

God's Little Angel

I'm God's little angel
Sent your way
To wish you
A happy Christmas Day!

—*Evangeline Carey*

King of Glory

Christ is born,
Our King of Glory,
Now you know
The Christmas story.

—*Robert Colbert*

God Turned on His Light

(Child turns on flashlight while speaking)

God turned on His light in a manger
One night so long ago.
It shone with heavenly glory
And set the world aglow.

—*Roma Joy Smith*

First Christmas Morn

On that first Christmas Morn
Christ, the Lord, was born.
Merry Christmas, everyone!

—*Robert Colbert*

God's Love Came Down

One lovely night, God's love came
down
Into a lowly place.
The glory of the Lord shone 'round
A little baby's face.

—*Roma Joy Smith*

God Is My Father

I love having God so near,
Sharing in a beautiful way.
I love Him as my Father
On this Christmas Day!

—*Evangeline Carey*

The World's Best Giver

God is the world's best giver.
He gives to everyone.
But His best gift—the very best—
The gift of His own Son.

—*Roma Joy Smith*

May Your Holiday Sparkle

May your holiday sparkle.
Yes, sing with joy,
Because God sent to us
His special Baby Boy . . .
Jesus Christ!

—*Evangeline Carey*

Rejoice

Rejoice! Rejoice!
It's Christmas morn,
Halle~~lujah! Rejoice~~
Ch~~~~

3

Jesus Is Born

Mary, sing your lullaby;
   Angels, wing your flight;
Shepherds, haste to Bethlehem;
   Wise men, see that light.
Jesus is born!

—Margaret Primrose

Heaven Blessed

Christmas is
The happiest time
Throughout the
Entire year.

And it's all because
Of Christ the Child,
Who brought us
Heaven's cheer!

—Robert Colbert

May God Bless Your Holiday

May your Christmas
   Be blessed by our Father above,
Who sent Jesus, His Child,
   In proof of His love!

Thank God for this gift
   More precious than I can tell.
God is indeed mighty
   And does all things well.

—Evangeline Carey

Christmas Means Giving

Christmas means giving
Because God gave to us.
So we should continue to give.
Let's share Jesus' love
With the people we meet
Everyday, for as long as we live.

—Brenda Wood

Happy Birthday, Little Jesus

Happy birthday, little Jesus,
   Lying in the hay.
Happy birthday, little Jesus,
   Born on Christmas Day.

Happy birthday, my Friend Jesus,
   Help me live each day
Like You did, my Friend Jesus,
   Born on Christmas Day.

—Wanda M. Trawick

Peace Would Abide

The spirit of this season
   Is reflected in each one
Who tries to follow God's rules
   Given to us by His Son.

If Jesus lived this Christmas
   In the hearts of all worldwide,
There would be love forever
   And with peace we would abide.

—Helen Kitchell Evans

Misunderstandings

I thought that Baby Jesus
Had an angel for a bed!
That's a very funny thing.
Did He have a nice, soft angel
To make a pillow for His head?
Or did He sleep on angel's wings?

But Daddy says it's not an angel.
It's a *manger* bed He had.
I never saw a manger.
I wonder if the Baby Jesus
Wished He had an angel
To make a pillow for His head.

—Marita M. Root

Star Reminder

(Sung to the tune of "Away in a Manger")

The stars twinkled brightly,
   That first Christmas night.
They told us of Jesus,
   The Truth and the Light.
Oh, may our hearts open,
   The Babe to recall.
The stars still remind us
   Of God's Gift to all.

—Enelle Eder

Let Us Worship

(Sung to the tune of "Silent Night")

Little Child, snug in the hay,
Shepherds came. Wise men prayed.
Angels sang of His holy birth.
Peace and joy to all those on earth.
Let us worship the King!
Let us worship the King!

—Enelle Eder

Rejoice and Sing

*(Sung to the tune of
"It Came upon a Midnight Clear")*

Rejoice, rejoice, rejoice and sing,
   The Son of God is come!
He laid aside His kingly crown
   And left His heavenly home.
In lowly cattle stall He lay,
   A manger for His bed.
In all the earth was found no room
   To lay His baby head.

—Enelle Eder

After Christmas

I got a ball for Christmas,
   But it's already flat.
My sister dropped her dolly,
   And that's the end of that.

We ate the pie and turkey;
   The Christmas tree looks dead;
The holiday is over
   Before we go to bed.

And yet it isn't over
   For Jesus is still here.
The peace and joy He brought us
   Will last from year to year.

—Margaret Primrose

For His Birthday

I got a brand-new ten-speed bike,
   My brother got a clarinet,
My little sister got a doll,
   But what did Jesus get?

Grandpa got a sweater,
   Grandma got a Scrabble set,
Cousin Billy got a boat,
   But what did Jesus get?

Daddy got a VCR,
   Mother got a ring,
But it was Jesus' birthday.
   Did He get anything?

—Wanda M. Trawick

Jesus' Birthday

When *I* have a birthday,
  Mother makes a cake,
All pink and white
With candles bright,
  The best that she can make.

And when *I* have a birthday,
  A party comes along,
With funny hats
And lots of gifts
  And a "Happy Birthday" song.

When *Jesus* has a birthday,
  We go to lots of fuss.
A tree we trim,
And we sing to Him,
  But we give the gifts to *us!*
(Child shrugs before leaving.)
  —*Marita M. Root*

Silver Bells

Silver bells are ringing,
Little children singing,
Jesus Christ is King!

Everyone comes together to rejoice,
The day our Lord and Savior was
  born!
Children are excited as they await
The miraculous return of the Lord!
For it is His birthday.

Silver bells ring
Everyone sing
Jesus Christ is King!

  —*Tenisha Younger*

What You Mean to Me

*(Child recites while looking
into a manger.)*

Little Baby in a manger,
  Just what do You mean to me?
Born so long ago it seemed that
  You and I should never meet.

But somebody told me that
  I was the reason for Your birth.
You loved me so very much;
  You came to live and die on earth.

Never sinning in Your life,
  You taught us all the way to live.
Dying for the sins of all,
  You now stand ready to forgive.

All we need to do is ask—
  The price for sin has all been paid.
When I heard of Your forgiveness,
  Then my life to You I gave.

So, little Baby in the manger,
  I want everyone to see,
You're my best Friend, Redeemer,
  Savior.
  You are everything to me!

  —*Brenda Wood*

6

Why Is Christmas Special?

Why is Christmas special?
  It's more than things we see—
The toys, the decorations,
  The lighted Christmas tree.

We love the smells of Christmas—
  Warm cookies on a tray,
The berry-scented candles,
  And earthy bed of hay.

The tastes are always tempting—
  The festive salad plates,
The turkey and the stuffing,
  The nuts, the pies, the dates.

We like the happy voices,
  The bells, the chimes, the choir,
The warmth of dying embers,
  The crackle of the fire.

But these are not the reason
  We celebrate each year.
They're not the things that bring us
  A special kind of cheer.

It only comes from Jesus,
  Who lives with God above
But left the joys of heaven
  To tell us of His love.

—Margaret Primrose

The Guiding Light

The Christmas star shone brightly
  Where the Baby Jesus lay
Cradled in a stable
  Upon sweet, new-mown hay.

"Follow me," it called,
  "Come and see the place."
So the wise men set out on camels
  To look upon Jesus' face.

The place where God selected
  For His only Son to be born.
The place where Jesus slept
  On that first Christmas morn.

The gift of His only Son
  Who would die on Calvary
To save us from our sins,
  People like you and me.

No gift will be as marvelous
  As the one God gave that night,
So at this Christmas season
  Let us follow that guiding light.

—Helen Kitchell Evans

Christmas Is Any Time

Christmas comes in winter
  When the ground is white,
But anytime is Christmas
  If our hearts are right.

It may come in April,
  March or June or May;
Morning, noon, or evening—
  Any time of day.

Christmas is believing
  In our Lord and King.
Christmas is receiving
  The joy He came to bring.

—Margaret Primrose

Exercises

Everywhere

(For seven children. Each child holds a large letter. The first four enter and hold up their letters chest high as they recite their lines. Then all together they raise them high over their heads. Second group of three enter and repeat the actions.)

"H" CHILD: Here we stand together,

"O" CHILD: Our love with you to share;

"P" CHILD: Please have a Merry Christmas,

"E" CHILD: Everywhere! Everywhere!

"J" CHILD: Just three little children,

"O" CHILD: Only three are we,

"Y" CHILD: Yet we bring great joy,

ALL: To friends and family.

—Helen Kitchell Evans

This Is the Reason

(For seven children. Arrange in a semicircle. Have children step forward to recite, then return to their places.)

1ST CHILD: Do you know why there is Christmas,
    Why we celebrate the day?

2ND CHILD: Do you often wonder about
    How it would feel to hear angels say,

3RD CHILD: "Glory to God in the highest,
    Peace on Earth among men!"

4TH CHILD: Do you know why Jesus came
    To this earth as a Baby Boy?

5TH CHILD: Do you often wonder why His name
    Gives so many people joy?

6TH CHILD: Well, here's the reason we praise Him
    And worship His holy name,
    Because He came for everyone,
    He loves us all the same.

7TH CHILD: He came to save us from our sins,
              To tell of His Father above;
              He came to give us all a chance
              To share in His heavenly love.

ALL: Yes, for *all* His life was given
              So that our sins might be forgiven.

                              —*Helen Kitchell Evans*

What a Gift!

(For two children. One is inside a box, wrapped for Christmas with a large hole at the top.)

1ST CHILD: This package looks important.
              I wonder what is in it?
              A peek inside will tell me.
              'Twill only take a minute.

2ND CHILD *(pokes head up from box):*
              I didn't want to scare you,
              But the gift inside is me,
              Although I'm not a present
              Wrapped to sit beneath a tree.

1ST CHILD: I guess that means there's something
              That you really want to do.
              You make it sound exciting.
              Will you let me play with you?

2ND CHILD: Perhaps I'd better tell you
              This is more than games and fun.
              I gave myself to Jesus
              And said, "Thanks, God, for Your Son."

1ST CHILD: Now you belong to Jesus,
              And how happy you must be.
              I'd really like to ask you—
              Is there room in there for me?

                              —*Margaret Primrose*

The Beauty of Christmas

(For four children)

1ST CHILD: Shining lights on the Christmas tree
              Give the room a special glow;

2ND CHILD: The star on the top makes us think
              Of the dear baby born long ago.

9

| 3RD CHILD: | The beautiful Christmas cards from friends, |
| | The greetings of joy and love; |

| 4TH CHILD: | All bring us thoughts of our Savior |
| | Who was sent from heaven above. |

ALL:	We want to live for Jesus,
	We want to do what is right,
	We want to show our love
	For the one who came Christmas night.

—Helen Kitchell Evans

After the Pageant

(For two children)

1ST CHILD:	I have question after question
	About the things I see.
	I've hardly heard of Jesus.
	His story's new to me.
	Why do you wear long, floppy clothes?
	A towel around your head?
	Why is your dolly in the hay?
	Doesn't it have a bed?

MARY:	I've tried to look like Mary did
	When Jesus came to earth.
	There was no inn that welcomed her
	The night she gave Him birth.

1ST CHILD:	Why did the girls all dress in white?
	There's tinfoil in their hair.
	What are those things that look like wings
	But don't go anywhere?

MARY:	Some angels flew to shepherd fields
	In robes of glistening white.
	Like them we sing of Christ, the King,
	Who came to us that night.

1ST CHILD:	What made the shepherds run so fast?
	Why did they leave their sheep?
	Couldn't they wait until sunrise?
	Didn't they need to sleep?

MARY:	I think they were so overjoyed
	That they just had to run.
	So off they went to find the Babe—
	God's One and Only Son.

1ST CHILD:	Who are the boys with cardboard crowns?
	What is that stuff they gave?
	Why did they march like kings and lords
	Then kneel like any slave?
MARY:	The wise men saw a brilliant star
	That led them to the King.
	They knelt to give the best they could,
	And that's what we should bring.

(Both children kneel. Have children's choir sing.)

—Margaret Primrose

The Nativity

(For seven children. Each child should bring a piece of the Nativity scene and add it to the set at the end of his or her speech. As an option, each child may hold a picture of the piece of the scene.)

1ST CHILD:	Angels filled the Christmas sky
	Bringing a message from on high.
2ND CHILD:	Mary sang that special day
	To her baby in the hay.
3RD CHILD:	Joseph watched his family with care
	Knowing that God had led them there.
4TH CHILD:	Shepherds came to worship Him.
	They followed the star to Bethlehem.
5TH CHILD:	Wise men traveled many miles
	To bring gifts to the holy Child.
6TH CHILD:	Animals bowed their heads down low
	To worship the Baby long ago.
7TH CHILD:	Gifts they gave from hearts of love
	To honor the tiny one sent from above.

—Enelle Eder

Christmas Is Special

(For four older children)

1ST CHILD:	Cookies make Christmas special.
	They smell so nice
	Filled with chocolate and nuts
	And lots of old-fashioned spice.
	(Holds up jar of cookies.)

11

2ND CHILD:	Family makes Christmas special; We sit around the tree. Dad tells the Christmas story To my little brother [sister] and me. *(Holds up large family picture.)*
3RD CHILD:	Grandparents make Christmas special; They bring so many things. I'm always very thankful For all that Christmas means. *(Points or waves to grandparents.)*
4TH CHILD:	Jesus makes Christmas special— Spreading love over all the earth; This is the time we celebrate His coming down to earth. *(Hold up picture of Jesus, or unroll a large poster of the Nativity.)*

—*Helen Kitchell Evans*

The Animals' Gifts

(For six older children. May be effectively combined with a Nativity scene. The narrator may introduce each animal, if desired.)

NARRATOR:	The animals gathered in the stable dim To discuss the gifts they brought to him.
DONKEY:	I carried sweet Mary To little Bethlehem town. I traveled surefooted, Up rocky roads and down.
COW:	I shared my rugged manger For the precious Baby's bed. I shared my tender hay To pillow His little head.
SHEEP:	I came from the hillside With shepherds of old. I gave my warm wool To shield Him from cold.
DOVE:	I watched the tiny Baby With sharp and careful eye. I cooed a lullaby song From my rafter up so high.
CAMEL:	I walked for many miles With wise men on my back To give the Christ child gifts I'd carried in my pack.

—*Enelle Eder*

Celebrate All Year

1ST CHILD: Let's pass on the glow of Christmas
To everyone we know;

2ND CHILD: Let's proclaim Christ's birth
Everywhere we go.

3RD CHILD: Let's let the joy of music
That seems to set us free
Overflow to others,
Our friends and family.

4TH CHILD: Let's keep that Christmas spirit
Captured within our heart,
And every day we live,
A bit of it impart.

5TH CHILD: Let's make Christmas daily living
Filled with joy and mirth;

ALL: Let's celebrate all year
The blessed Savior's birth.

—Helen Kitchell Evans

The Christmas Stars

(Each should hold a large, brightly colored star with the key word written on it.)

1ST STAR: This is the star of FAITH,
Kept by men of long ago.
They knew the Savior would come
Because God told them so.

2ND STAR: This is the star of PEACE,
Brought on the first Christmas Day,
But its message is still the same,
He came to light our way.

3RD STAR: This is the star of HOPE,
Sent from up above;
Its rays will fill our hearts
With God's abiding love.

4TH STAR: This is the star of JOY,
The angels brought to earth,
Joyous news to all
Of Baby Jesus' birth.

5TH STAR:	This is the star of LOVE
	For everyone on the earth.
	God sent His only Son
	To a lowly, humble birth.
6TH STAR:	This is the star of GOODWILL,
	Its rays are never dim.
	Angels sang from the skies,
	"Welcome the Babe of Bethlehem."
ALL:	All the stars hold a message true
	Of a wonderful Savior
	Sent for me and you!

—*Enelle Eder*

The Best Time of the Year

(For two groups, possibly a split-choir.
Solo parts should vary in tone, rising and falling for effect.)

1ST GROUP:	The best time of the year is Christmas.
2ND GROUP:	There's no doubt about it.
SOLO 1:	It's when we all hope for gifts.
SOLO 2:	If we've been good or bad, we sure find out!
1ST GROUP:	The best time of the year is Christmas.
2ND GROUP:	Carols fill the air!
SOLO 3:	There's a hush *(hushed voice)* and whisper.
SOLO 4:	We hear it everywhere.
1ST GROUP:	The best time of the year is Christmas.
2ND GROUP:	Not because of all the above.
SOLO 5:	It's because Jesus came.
SOLO 6:	He brought to us His love.
1ST GROUP:	The best time of the year is Christmas.
2ND GROUP:	It's the birthday of Jesus, our King!
SOLO 7:	All praise be given to Jesus!
SOLO 8:	Great blessings does He bring!

ALL: The best time of the year is Christmas.
Let us sing and show our joy!
God's precious gift is Christmas,
The birth of His Son; God's holy *(pause)* Baby Boy.
Let us praise and sing our joy!
(CHORUS *sings, perhaps joined by a children's choir.)*

—*Helen Kitchell Evans*

Praise the Son

(For a split-choir. Solo parts should vary in tone, rising and falling for effect.)

ALL: *(Sing: "O Thou Joyful, O Thou Wonderful" or other)*

1ST GROUP: God is . . .

SOLO 1: Sustainer,

SOLO 2: Creator,

SOLO 3: Lord God,

1ST GROUP: And Savior.

3RD GROUP: Everything,
Everyone,
Everywhere,
Praise the Son!

2ND GROUP: Righteous and holy,

SOLO 4: Forgiving and kind,

SOLO 5: Jesus is ruler
Over heart and mind.

1ST and 3RD GROUP:
Justice and mercy,
Go hand in hand;
Offers salvation
To each woman and man.

2ND GROUP: Everything,
Everyone,
Everywhere,
Praise the Son!

1ST and 3RD GROUP:
>   Of His birth angels

SOLO 6:   Sang the great news,

SOLO 7:   "Jesus has come,
>   For me and for you."

2ND and 3RD GROUP:
>   Come as a child,
>   Heralded by a star
>   That brought wise men,
>   The magi from afar.

3RD GROUP: Everything,
>   Everyone,
>   Everywhere,
>   Praise the Son!

ALL: *(Sing: "Hark! the Herald Angels Sing" or other)*

1ST GROUP: Come to deliver
>   People from sin,
>   If only we'll listen,

SOLO 8:   *(softly)* And let Him in.

3RD GROUP: Into a life,
>   Of hurt and despair,
>   Letting God's love
>   Instead, reside there.

1ST GROUP: Everything,

2ND GROUP: Everyone,

3RD GROUP: Everywhere,

ALL: Praise the Son!

1ST GROUP: For God is . . .

SOLO 1:   Sustainer,

SOLO 2:   Creator,

SOLO 3:   Lord God

1ST GROUP: And Savior.

16

2ND GROUP: Righteous and holy,

SOLO 4:   Forgiving and kind,

SOLO 5:   Jesus is ruler
                        Over heart and mind.

3RD GROUP: Justice and mercy,
                      Go hand in hand;
                         Offers salvation
                 To each woman and man.

ALL: Everything!
                     Everyone!
                        Everywhere!
                 Praise the Son!

                              —C. R. Scheidies

Sketches

The Animals' Christmas

By Enelle Eder

CAST:
> Donkey
> Cow
> Sheep 1
> Curly
> Sheep 2
> Sheep 3
> Mary, nonspeaking
> Joseph, nonspeaking

PROPS:
> Hay bales, manger

PRODUCTION NOTES:
> Any number of persons may be used. Add extra animals to the barn scene. Also, extras may be used as part of a choir at appropriate times if desired. Elaborate costuming is not necessary; something as simple as a hood with appropriate colors and ears may suffice. Place bales of hay around stage to suggest a barn. Other areas of the room may be used for shepherd scenes. Use lighting to help with transitions.

Scene 1

(Lights up on stable. Cow, Sheep 1, and other animals are in stable.)

Donkey *(entering):* Ohhh. My aching back!

(Others watch as Donkey enters and finds a comfortable place. Cow moves over to Donkey.)

Cow: Excuse me, but what are you doing in our barn?

Donkey: Oh, I'm looking for a good place to rest my aching bones.

Cow: But you can't stay here. This is *our* barn. Besides, it's already too crowded in here.

DONKEY: Sure I can. The man at the inn said we could all stay here.

SHEEP 1: All? You mean there are more animals coming?

DONKEY: No, not animals. People.

COW: People! Now I've heard it all. People do not stay in barns.

DONKEY: Well, they are going to tonight, because the innkeeper said his rooms were full, but we could sleep in the stable. Besides, Mary cannot go any farther tonight, and the baby could come anytime now, anytime at all, and . . .

SHEEP 1: Baby? Baby? Oh dear, this is awful!

COW: What *are* you talking about?

DONKEY: Did I forget to tell you about the baby? You see, that is why my back is killing me. I carried Mary all the way from Nazareth, and she is going to have a baby.

COW: We simply cannot have a baby born in our barn!

DONKEY: Well I agree that it is no place for the Messiah to be born, but I . . .

SHEEP 1: Oh dear. Oh dear! Did you say the Messiah? Oh dear!

COW: Now what are you talking about?

DONKEY: Did I forget to mention the angel that came to Mary and told her that her son would be Christ, the King: the Messiah?

COW: Yes! You did forget to mention that! This will never do. A stable is no place for a baby, and especially no place for the Christ child.

SHEEP 1: Oh dear. I think I'm going to faint.

(Lights darken on stable. Add choir singing "Away in a Manger" verses 1 and 2 if desired. MARY *and* JOSEPH *join the stable scene.)*

Scene 2

(Lights up on the field and CURLY, SHEEP 2, *and* SHEEP 3*)*

CURLY: Hey! Wait up, you guys. Where are you going in such a hurry?

SHEEP 2: We are on our way to Bethlehem. Didn't you hear the angels singing and telling the shepherds about the birth of the Messiah?

CURLY: I guess I was sort of sleeping.

SHEEP 3: How could you sleep through that! Come on, Curly, we don't want to miss out on seeing the Baby.

CURLY: You mean that we have to walk all the way to Bethlehem just to see a baby?

SHEEP 2: Not just a baby. It's the promised Messiah, and the angels said He has been sent to save His people.

CURLY: But how are we going to find Him?

SHEEP 3: The angels said to follow that big, bright star up there, and it will lead us to the right place. I bet it's someplace special and beautiful.

CURLY (looking around before speaking): Ah, I hate to tell you guys this, but that star has just stopped over a barn.

(Lights dim slowly. Choir may sing if desired. CURLY, SHEEP 2, and SHEEP 3 join the others in the stable.)

Scene 3

(Lights up on stable)

COW: Just look at the tiny little thing. Can't you just see how special He is?

DONKEY: I heard someone say He is the Son of God.

COW: But why would God want His Son to be born in an animal barn?

DONKEY: The angels were singing about God loving us so much that he sent His Son as a gift to us. I wish I had a gift to give back to Him.

COW: Well, let's give it some thought. (All pause to think, then to DONKEY) You know, you did a big job by carrying Mary all the way here on your back so that she wouldn't have to walk. That could be considered sort of a gift.

DONKEY: I suppose you are right. Maybe each one of us doing our part would be like gifts we could give.

(Add song if desired, possibly "I Said the Donkey." Animals gently move in closer to crowd around the manger.)

CURLY: I know that we animals shouldn't be so close to the Baby, but I just have to get a closer look. There is such a strange feeling in the air tonight.

COW: I know what you mean. I feel it too.

DONKEY: Just look at Mary and Joseph's faces. They look so peaceful and full of love. They almost glow.

CURLY: Who would think that one little child could bring such love and peace to everyone who meets Him?

DONKEY: I don't know how to explain it, but if He truly is the Messiah, the Savior, He certainly could.

COW: Look! I think He's smiling at us. It's like . . . It's like He even cares about us animals. Just think how much He must love His people.

CURLY: You know, I do believe it. I believe He is the Messiah!

DONKEY: So do I. I'll never forget this moment. I'm glad He came.

COW: Imagine. The king being born right here in our stable. He deserves to be worshiped and adored.

(Close with a song or lights out)

Christmas in the Hayloft

by Margaret Primrose

CAST:
> ALAN, a preteen boy
> MEGAN, his sister
> JEFF, Alan's cousin
> KIM, Jeff's sister
> GRANDPA

PROPS:
> Sleeping bags, bales of hay, Thermos, and cups.

PRODUCTION NOTES:
> Use as elaborate or minimal staging as desired.

Scene One

(Lights up. JEFF *enters carrying sleeping bag. He hears a bang on the wall away from him.)*

JEFF: Alan! What was that?

ALAN *(enters with sleeping bag):* I don't know, but I don't like it. *(Another bang.)* There it is again. Somewhere downstairs. It would help if that one little window let in more light.

JEFF: I know.

(They hear a whinny.)

ALAN *(laughing):* It's just the pony kicking the wall. He's tied in the stall, and we're disturbing him. He'll calm down in a little bit.

JEFF: I hope so.

ALAN: Do you suppose the animals in the stable with Mary and Joseph acted like that?

JEFF: Yes, I do.

ALAN: Well, I think this spot is as good as any to try out our new sleeping bags. (JEFF *sneezes.)* What's the matter? Are you catching cold?

JEFF: No, but the dust in this hay makes me sneeze.

ALAN: Well, I guess we didn't expect it to be as clean as a hospital.

JEFF: Do you suppose there are any mice in the hay?

ALAN: Probably not many. Grandpa always keeps a cat in the barn to scare them away.

(They spread out their sleeping bags.)

JEFF: Well, are we ready to crawl in?

ALAN: Aren't you even going to take off your shoes?

JEFF: Maybe, but I think I'd rather be prepared if we have to hurry out of here. I wish we'd brought some water to drink.

ALAN: You could go downstairs to the faucet. This isn't like Bethlehem where there were only wells.

JEFF: No, I'll wait. *(He sneezes again.)* What I really need is a tissue. I can't find mine in the dark.

ALAN: Well, I brought a birthday candle *(lights it)* and some matches for an emergency.

JEFF: Alan, you can't use matches where there's hay. It burns too easily.

ALAN: Help me, Jeff. I just dropped one that was smoking. If we don't stamp it out fast, we may be in big trouble.

JEFF: I know. *(They stamp the floor vigorously.)* Grandpa says hay can smoke a long time before it burns. Dust, mice, darkness, a pony that doesn't want to be here. What next? Let's go to the house.

ALAN: No. Don't you see? They are just some of the little problems Mary and Joseph must have had.

JEFF: I guess you're right, and they didn't have anywhere else to go. *(They hear a sliding door.)* What's that?

ALAN: Sounds like the door sliding open.

JEFF: I'm scared. What do we do now?

ALAN: I don't know.

GRANDPA *(offstage)*: Boys!

ALAN: It's Grandpa. Pretend you're asleep. If he comes up here and finds out we had matches, he'll tell our parents.

JEFF: Yeah, and he always seems to know things like that.

GRANDPA: Jeff? Alan? It's Grandpa. Is everything all right up there?

23

JEFF: Sure. It is now.

GRANDPA: I decided to bring my sleeping bag, too, and spend the night in the barn with you. If that's all right.

JEFF: You know it is. I guess we'll both feel safer if you're here with us.

GRANDPA *(entering with Thermos and cups):* Are you chilly? I brought some hot cider. Everyone at the house is having some before going to bed.

ALAN: Hot cider! I guess Mary and Joseph didn't have anything that good at the stable.

GRANDPA: Probably not. And I'm sure they didn't have a Thermos either. But the Bible doesn't say that they had nothing good to eat or drink. It just says there wasn't any room for them at the inn. *(He pours.)*

JEFF: Thanks, Grandpa.

ALAN: Thanks. Mmmm'm. This is good.

GRANDPA: Has coming out here tonight helped you understand the Christmas story a little better than before?

JEFF: Yes, but it's not really very much fun.

GRANDPA: It was a time of great joy, but Mary and Joseph's joy didn't depend on having everything perfect. Well, it's getting late. Would you rather put your new sleeping bags on the living floor? If I know you two, you'll try to be the first ones at the Christmas tree in the morning.

ALAN: No, I'll stick it out.

JEFF: I'm staying too. This place will keep us from oversleeping, and what does it matter if the girls see their presents first? Mary and Joseph didn't even have a Christmas tree.

(Lights out)

Scene Two

(Lights up)

KIM *(calling from offstage):* Jeff, is it all right if Megan and I come up?

JEFF *(sits up and looks around):* Yes. Come on up.

KIM *(entering):* Do you have any idea where Alan went?

JEFF: No. I just woke up. Aren't he and Grandpa in the house?

MEGAN: Grandpa is, but Alan isn't. The pony's gone too. Did you hear anything in the night?

JEFF: No. *(He jumps up.)* Maybe Grandpa should call the police.

MEGAN: He wants to look around the farm first.

JEFF: You don't suppose somebody kidnapped Alan, do you?

KIM: Things like that seldom happen out here in the country.

JEFF: Maybe we can find some tracks to follow.

KIM: I doubt it, the ground's frozen solid.

JEFF: Won't Alan get awfully cold if he's riding the pony somewhere?

MEGAN: I'm afraid so. Hey, what is this burned-out match doing on the floor?

JEFF: Well *(pause)* Alan had it last night.

MEGAN: Does Grandpa know about it? Maybe Alan ran away because he couldn't find it and was afraid Grandpa would.

KIM: Look here. There's a tiny bit of burned hay too.

MEGAN: Well, if I set fire to the barn, I'd run away too.

JEFF: Oh, don't be so hard on him. The barn's all right. *(They hear the door slide open.)* Alan! Where have you been?

ALAN *(from offstage):* I'll tell you after I tie up the pony.

KIM *(as ALAN enters):* You really gave us a scare.

ALAN: Well, I woke up and couldn't go back to sleep, so . . .

MEGAN: You worried about what would happen when Mom and Dad found out you were playing with matches.

ALAN: Matches? *(Groans)* Oh, no!

MEGAN: I'm telling.

ALAN: Just like a sister.

KIM: Well, I'm your cousin, not your sister, and I think it would be better if you told Grandpa.

JEFF: I agree with my sister for once.

(They hear the door slide open.)

GRANDPA *(calling from offstage):* Jeff, are you awake?

JEFF: Yes. The girls and Alan are up here too.

GRANDPA *(enters):* Well, Alan, I guess you decided to take a little ride before anyone else was up. But don't you think you should have told us.

ALAN: Uh . . . yes. I'm sorry, Grandpa.

GRANDPA: You're forgiven.

ALAN: There's . . . something else I should tell you. I dropped a match last night before you came to the barn. Jeff and I had to work pretty hard to make sure it was out. Here are the rest of the matches. I promise I won't do that again.

GRANDPA: Good enough! But why did you run away?

ALAN: I started pretending you were Herod.

KIM: Herod? Grandpa's nothing like him.

ALAN: I know, but Mary and Joseph had to escape from Herod to save Baby Jesus' life.

MEGAN: So you ran away in the middle of the night?

ALAN: Well, not far. Just to the hog house.

JEFF: At least it's warm enough there with a sleeping bag.

ALAN: Yes, but running away was scary. I could almost hear Herod's men chasing me. I won't do that again either.

GRANDPA: It sounds like you've been reading about Tom Sawyer and Huckleberry Finn. What's more important, you've been thinking about the greatest story ever told. Well, merry Christmas, kids! Let's go back to the house.

Let Your Star So Shine

by Ron Hilligas

CAST:
> NARRATOR
> STARLA
> SCOOTER
> A DEEP VOICE
> TWINKLE
> STARLIGHT
> STARBRIGHT

PROPS:
> None needed

PRODUCTION NOTES:
> The scene takes place in the heavens. Use as minimal or elaborate staging and costumes as desired. If you have an advanced roller-skater, use him or her as SCOOTER.

(With lights down, musical background plays, "Angels We Have Heard on High" or other.)

NARRATOR: In the beginning God created the heavens and the earth. *(Pause)* Then God said, "Let there be light," and there was light. And God saw the light, that it was good. He created the sun for the day, and for the night he created the moon and all the stars. Big stars, little stars, bright stars, and even the stars that do not seem to twinkle as bright as others. *(Pause)* Like the star named Starla-la-East. *(Music fades as lights come up.)*

STARLA *(entering):* Oh, I wish I could shine bright, and twinkle up in the sky like my friends. They are so beautiful and I . . . well . . . I feel so dull.

TWINKLE: Hi, Starla! Have you seen Starlight and Starbright?

STARLA: No, Twinkle Twinkle, why?

TWINKLE: I just heard some kids sing a song about me, and I wanted them to hear it.

STARLA: They sang a song about you?

TWINKLE: Yep. It goes like this . . . (He sings "Twinkle, Twinkle, Little Star.")

(STARLIGHT *and* STARBRIGHT *enter while* TWINKLE *sings.*)

STARLIGHT *(interrupting):* What are you doing?

TWINKLE: Singing my song.

STARBRIGHT: Your song?

TWINKLE: The kids sing a song to me. *(He continues his song.)*

STARLIGHT: That's great! But, they also have a poem for us. It goes like this. Starlight . . .

STARBRIGHT: Starbright . . .

STARLIGHT and STARBRIGHT: First star I see tonight. I wish I may, I wish I might, have the wish I wish tonight.

TWINKLE: Wonderful! Let's tell Scooter about this.

(STARLIGHT, STARBRIGHT, *and* TWINKLE *exit, singing and reciting.*)

NARRATOR: Now Starla had many friends, but her best friend was Scooter, a shooting star.

SCOOTER *(shoots in):* Hi, Starla. What are you doing?

STARLA: I'm trying to shine brighter, like those other stars.

SCOOTER: Like who?

STARLA: Like Twinkle, Starlight, and Starbright.

SCOOTER: What for?

STARLA: Well . . . they have songs and poems written about them. I want to be popular just like them.

SCOOTER: Oh, Starla, I think you are a very special star. You are my best friend, but sometimes you act like a dimwit.

STARLA *(hurt):* Why? What do you mean?

SCOOTER: God made each of us special. We are all unique, one of a kind. Starlight and Starbright like to take turns getting up first, so they can hear their poem. Twinkle has a special twinkler that makes kids want to sing her [him] a song.

STARLA: Yeah, and God gave you roller skates so you can skate across the sky. But what about me? God didn't make me special.

SCOOTER: Yes, He did. You're special because you are full of love, Starla, and that is more important than being flashy like the others.

STARLA: Thanks for trying to cheer me up, Scooter, but I feel duller all the time. Who likes a dull star like me? Please just leave me alone! *(She exits, crying.)*

*(*TWINKLE *enters.)*

TWINKLE: Have you seen Starla?

SCOOTER *(pointing):* She went that way. Why?

TWINKLE: God wants to see her.

SCOOTER *(amazed):* Really? What for?

TWINKLE: I don't know, but we were told to hurry and find her.

(They exit. STARLIGHT *and* STARBRIGHT *enter.)*

STARLIGHT: Starla, oh Starla!

STARBRIGHT: Come out, come out, wherever you are.

STARLIGHT: I'll bet she's in *big* trouble.

STARBRIGHT: Why else would *He* want to see her?

STARLIGHT: God's probably upset that she is so dull and doesn't sparkle.

(They exit, still calling for STARLA. STARLA *enters.)*

STARLA: Sometimes I wish I was a planet. They have cool names, and get to be in songs and . . .

DEEP VOICE: Starla.

STARLA: Y . . . yes?

DEEP VOICE: Starla, listen to Me.

STARLA: Who . . . what do You want, Lord?

DEEP VOICE: Starla, I have a very important job for you.

STARLA *(surprised):* You do?

DEEP VOICE: Yes, Starla. Soon I will send a very special gift to earth, and I need your help to announce that this gift has arrived.

STARLA: How can I help? I'm sort of . . . well . . . dull.

DEEP VOICE: Oh, Starla. My gift to earth is a gift of love . . . My love. You are the only star that has this special kind of love. That is the way I made *you*. When you shine with this love, you will be the brightest star ever.

STARLA: Oh. *(Pause)* When do you want me to shine?

DEEP VOICE: You will know when to shine.

(STARLA *nods her head and exits.*)

NARRATOR: Days went by until one night something special happened. The heavens bustled with excitement.

(ALL STARS *except* STARLA *enter.*)

SCOOTER: What's going on?

TWINKLE: I heard God is giving a gift to earth.

STARBRIGHT: It must be something pretty special. I heard the angel choir rehearsing.

STARLIGHT: Yes, what a glorious sound.

SCOOTER: Has anyone seen Starla?

STARLIGHT: I haven't.

(A bright, shiny STARLA *enters.)*

TWINKLE: Neither have . . . wow! Look at that star!

STARBRIGHT: That is the most beautiful, spectacular, brilliant star I have ever seen.

STARLIGHT: Where did *she* come from?

SCOOTER: It can't be . . . It's Starla! *(All react with amazement.)* What happened to you, Starla?

STARLA: Later tonight, God is giving a special gift of love to earth, and I get to announce this gift by shining over the town of Bethlehem. I get to shine over the newborn Savior of the whole world.

TWINKLE: But . . . why you?

STARLA *(humble but happy):* God said it was because He made me with love. It is that special love that makes me shine like this.

SCOOTER: Oh, Starla, I'll bet now you'll have songs and poems written about you.

STARLA: That's all right, Scooter, I don't need that now . . . not when I can shine for Him.

NARRATOR: Sure enough, many songs and poems have been written about Starla-la-east, because it was she that the Bible says, [read Matthew 2:9-10]. Remember, like Starla here, you are special to God. If you have His love in you, love for God and His Son Jesus, you, too, will shine like Starla-la-east.

(Spotlight focuses on STARLA, *the rest fade into background. Close with the cast singing an appropriate song, or possibly lead into a Nativity scene with* STARLA *as the star of Bethlehem.)*

Born for All

by Deborah Taylor

CAST:
>MARY
>JOHN, a shepherd boy
>AMOS, an elderly shepherd
>JOSEPH

PROPS:
>Manger, doll (for Baby Jesus)

PRODUCTION NOTES:
>The scene is set inside the stable at Bethlehem. Any dark setting would suffice, so long as the actors maintain the illusion of a room.

(Lights up on MARY *in middle of room)*

MARY: Joseph? Joseph? *(Runs to window)* Only more shepherds. What are they doing here? *(She goes to manger and picks up baby, holding him tight.)* Don't worry. Don't worry, sweet baby. We're fine. Mommy will watch out for You. Mommy's here. You're safe. Those shepherds won't bother You. *(Puts baby down in manger)* Oh, Joseph, where are you? What's taking so long? We need you here with us more than we need food to eat. *(Returns to window)* So many of them. All just kneeling, praying . . . what do they want? *(Looks at baby)* I know what they want, all right. Everything's been so strange with Him, right from the start. *(She moves over to the manger again.)* Well, they can't have Him. He's here, now, and He's mine. He's my sweet, precious, darling, beautiful baby boy, and I'm not going to let a lot of strangers near Him. *(A knock. Mary moves to the door and speaks hopefully yet tentatively.)* Joseph?

AMOS *(from outside / offstage)*: No, ma'am.

MARY: I won't speak with anyone until Joseph returns.

AMOS: Ma'am . . .

JOHN *(also from outside / offstage)*: Can't we see Him? Please?

AMOS: We've come so far.

JOHN: Please. The angels said we could see Him.

MARY *(fearful):* Angels?

AMOS: Please let us in. There are only two of us, an old man and a little boy.

MARY: What about the others?

AMOS: Just us.

(MARY *starts to open the door, stops, then runs over to the manger. She picks up the baby carefully, clutching him tightly. She moves back to the door and unlocks it.*)

JOHN: It's Him.

AMOS: The Savior. Praise God.

JOHN: Praise God.

(JOHN *and* AMOS *kneel and remain so for an uncomfortable length of time.*)

MARY *(perplexed):* Aren't you going to get up?

AMOS: I could stay like this, sharing His presence, worshiping Him, until I die.

JOHN: Me too.

MARY: No. Please get up.

(AMOS *and* JOHN *rise.* JOHN *inches his way slightly closer to the baby.*)

JOHN: Can I see Him?

MARY *(initially clutches baby tighter, then relaxes):* Certainly, child. Come closer.

(MARY *holds the baby so that both* JOHN *and* AMOS *can see.* JOHN *and* AMOS *move closer.*)

AMOS: My Lord and my God.

JOHN: Pretty. So pretty.

MARY *(proudly):* He is, isn't He?

JOHN: May I hold Him?

MARY: Oh, I don't think so.

JOHN: Please? I know how to hold a baby. My mama has had three babies, and she lets me hold them. She even let me take care of them all by myself, once.

MARY: Well, I guess . . .

(MARY *hands the child over carefully.* JOHN *is solemn as he takes the baby and stares at Him.*)

JOHN: The Savior. The one for whom angels sang.

AMOS *(looking over* JOHN's *shoulder):* Praise God. *(To* MARY) We've come a long way. There are others outside.

MARY: So many others.

JOHN: Please let me take Him outside. I've proved I'm not going to hurt Him.

MARY: No, I don't think so. Maybe you should give Him back.

JOHN: Please? He likes me. He's smiling at me. You can watch me the whole time. Please?

AMOS: The angels said we could all see Him. All of us. That's why we traveled so far.

JOHN: You'll let me take Him, won't you?

MARY: I'll carry Him out myself.

JOHN: Awww, but He likes me. See? Can't I please? Won't you share? You can watch me the whole time.

(Silence)

MARY: Take Him, then, but be careful, mind you.

(JOHN *exits with the baby.* MARY *sinks down and covers her face to hide her tears.*)

AMOS: Don't worry. He won't be hurt.

MARY *(in a broken voice):* I know.

AMOS: That isn't what bothers you, is it?

MARY: No. He's my baby. *Mine!* He's supposed to be mine!

AMOS: Now, now. Don't take on so. He's yours. You just don't understand.

MARY: Understand what?

AMOS: Children, they're never really yours. Never. The first time they want to do what you don't want them to do, or think what you don't want them to think, then you know they aren't really yours at all. Children belong to themselves. All a parent can ever do is try to teach and protect. But this one . . . this one is different. He is yours. He's yours, and He's mine. He's the Savior, and He's here for us.

34

MARY: So my baby . . .

AMOS: Really is your baby. Our baby. *(Gestures toward the audience)* And theirs. More than any other child could ever be.

MARY: Here for all of us. Not really to share . . .

AMOS: But for each of us to claim as being completely our very own. Each of us.

MARY: A son that isn't mine and never could be wholly mine . . .

AMOS: But better yet . . .

MARY: A Savior that is mine . . .

AMOS: And always will be.

(JOSEPH *enters carrying a basket of food.)*

JOSEPH: Mary?

MARY: It's all right.

JOSEPH: Mary, who are those men? Where's the baby?

MARY: It's all right, Joseph. Everything is all right.

JOSEPH: How . . .

MARY *(with a tear and a smile):* Rejoice, for unto you is born this day . . . a Savior.

(Lights out)

Christmas
Program Builder
No. 47

Resources for Christmas Programs

Recitations ● Exercises ● Sketches

Compiled by Paul M. Miller

KANSAS CITY, MO 64141

CONTENTS